Zoé de Las Cases

SECRET PARIS

Color Your Way to Calm

Little, Brown and Company

New York   Boston   London

Little, Brown and Company
Hachette Book Group
1290 Avenue of the Americas, New York, NY 10104
littlebrown.com

First North American Edition: June 2015
Originally published as *Paris Secret* in France by Éditions Marabout, August 2014

Little, Brown and Company is a division of Hachette Book Group, Inc.
The Little, Brown name and logo are trademarks of Hachette Book Group, Inc.

The publisher is not responsible for websites (or their content) that are not owned by the publisher.

The Hachette Speakers Bureau provides a wide range of authors for speaking events. To find out more, go to hachettespeakersbureau.com or call (866) 376-6591.

ISBN 978-0-316-26582-9
Library of Congress Control Number: 2015938249

10 9 8 7 6 5 4

WW

Printed in the United States of America

Zoé de Las Cases is the artistic director of a creative agency in Paris.

THIS BOOK BELONGS TO:

....

WELCOME
TO MY SECRET PARIS!

A Paris in black and white is just waiting for you and your colored pencils to bring it to life. It's time to restore the City of Light to all its colorful glory!

Join me in discovering a secret Paris: a city of fashion and a way of life that inspires people all over the world. Follow me through the picturesque streets, stopping here and there to admire the beautiful buildings and the stylish shops. As dusk descends, cross the Seine and stroll along its banks, or relax in a local bistro with a glass of wine.

Our walk ends on the rooftop terraces of the French capital. The sun is setting, and in the distance you can just make out the Eiffel Tower.

My palette ranges from soft pastel shades to bright, vivid colors, not to mention the sepia tones of years gone by. What colors will you choose?

Now pick up your pencils and give free rein to your imagination as you let your Parisian dreams carry you away!

Let the spirit of Paris be your guide.

Under the Paris sky

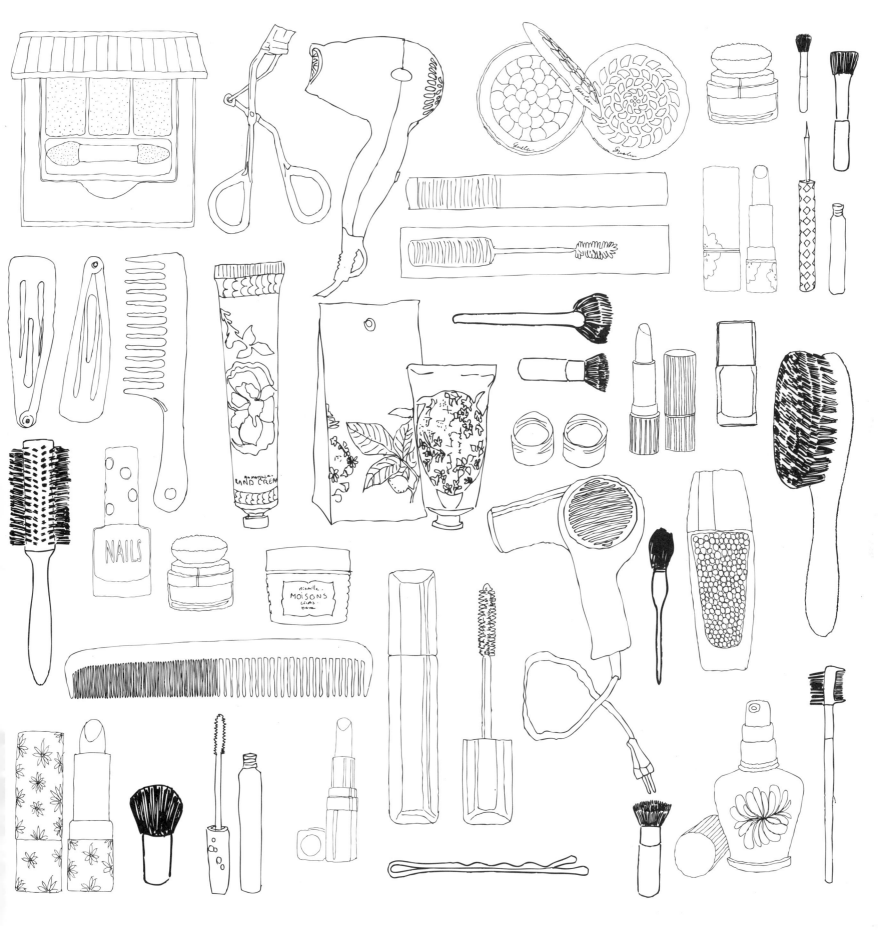

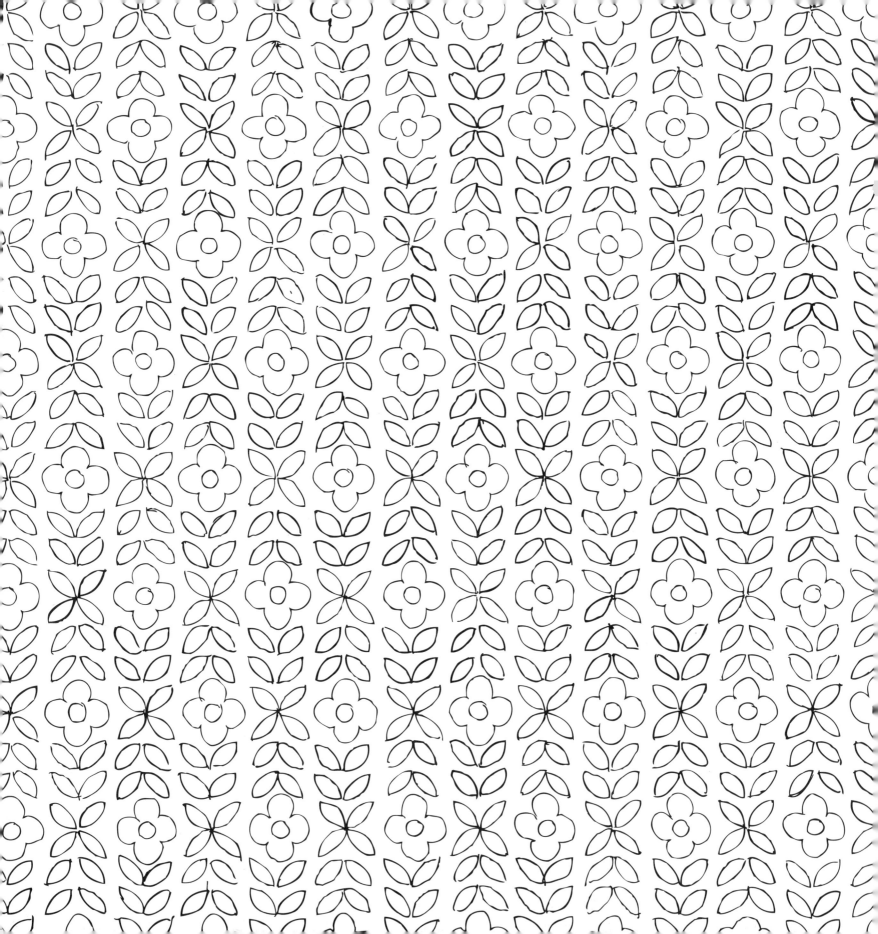

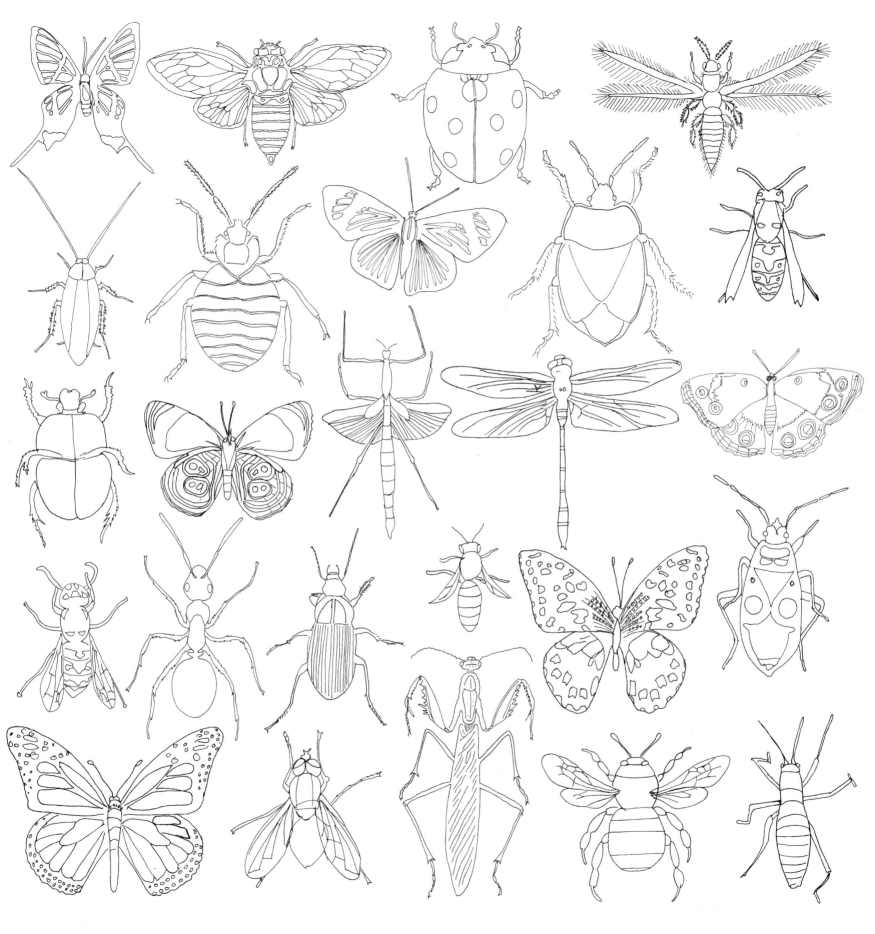

A Parisian pigeon

my little haberdashery

BOINH
FRANCE

A small cup of tea?

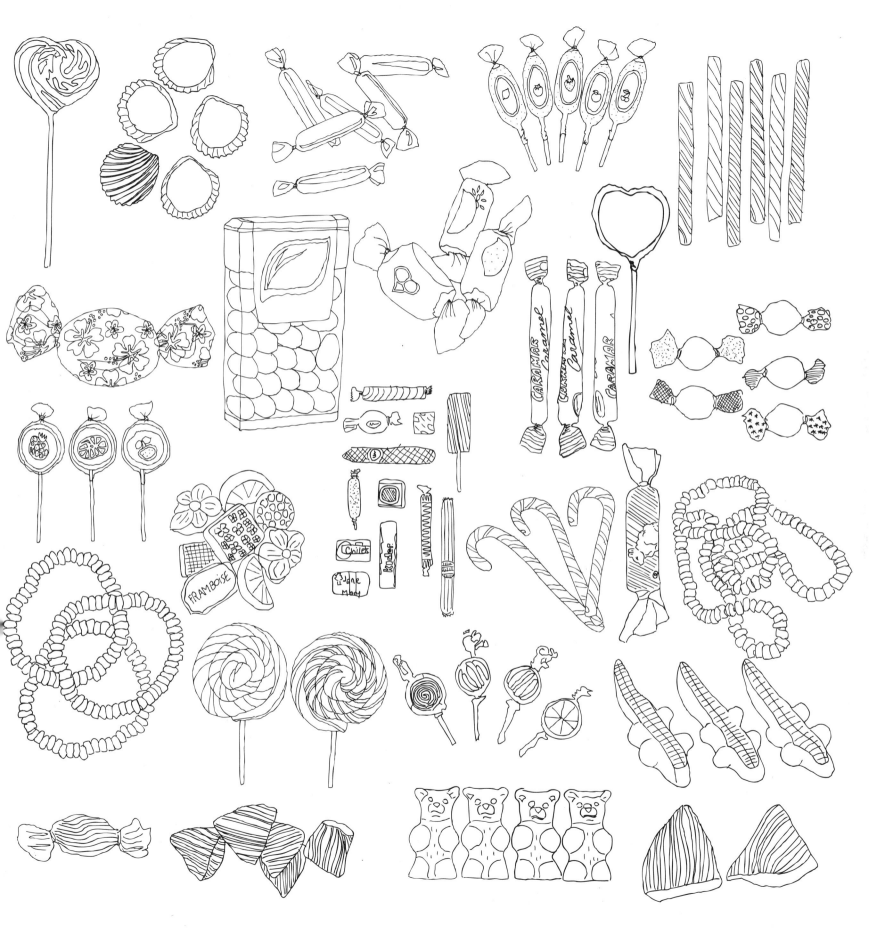

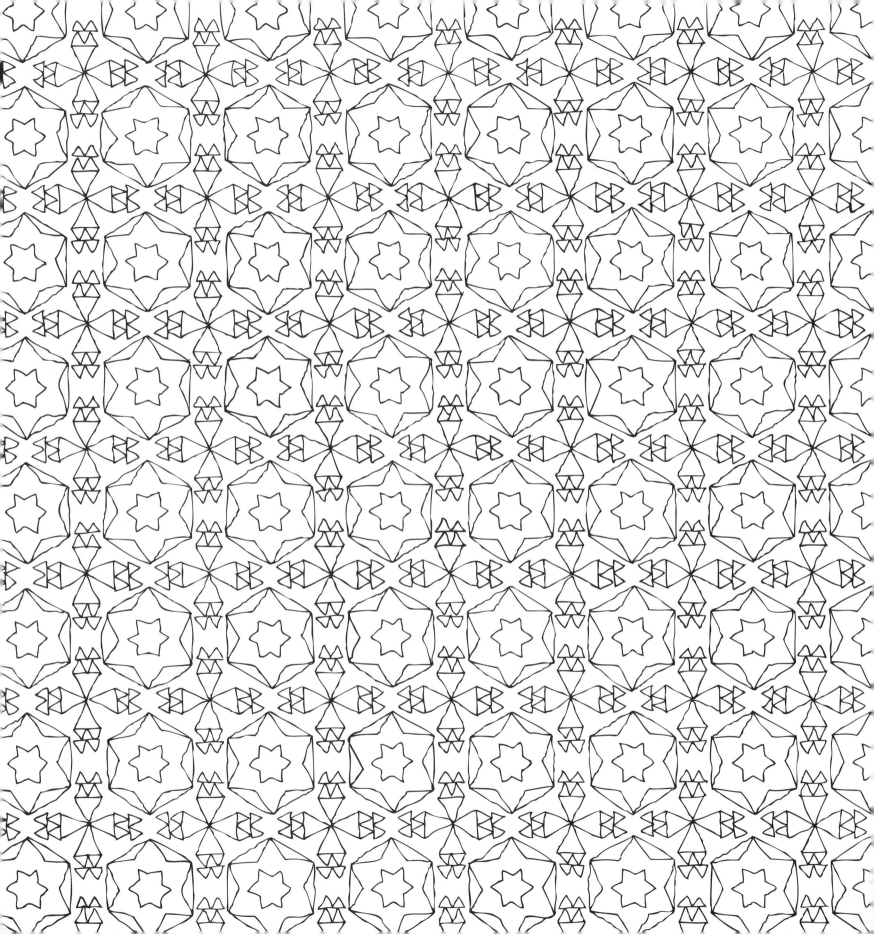

BONJOUR

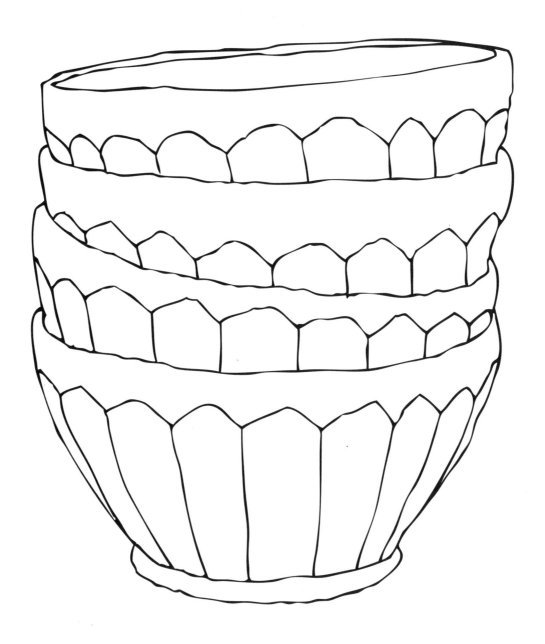

COFFEE

TEA

SUGAR

VANILLA

SUGAR FLOUR COOK

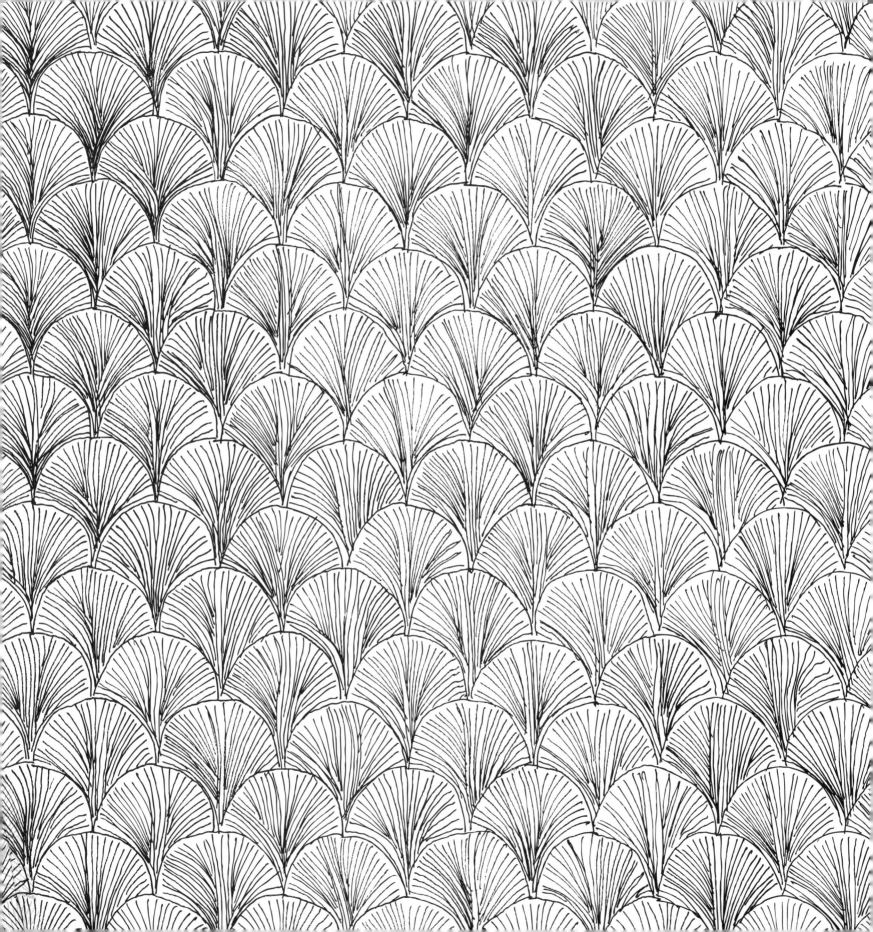

LEGUMES FRAIS

Tomates   3,80 * le kg
Asperges   4,50 * le kg
Haricots   6,80 * le kg
Carottes   1,80 * le kg
Endives   8,80 * le kg
Courgettes 0,80 * le kg

A coffee, please

La vie en Rose

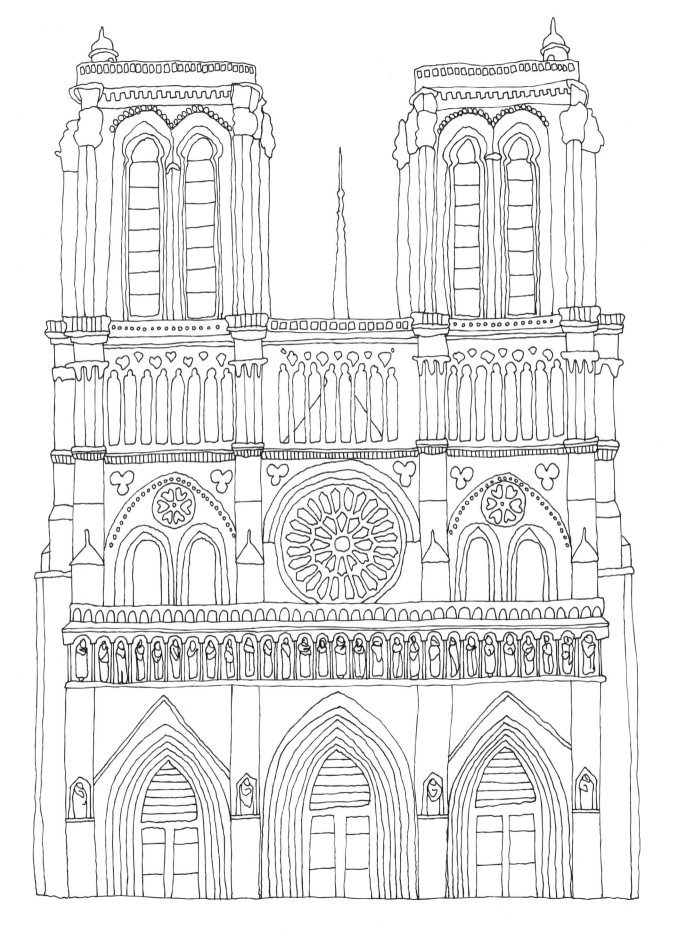

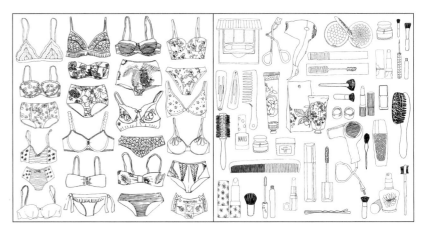

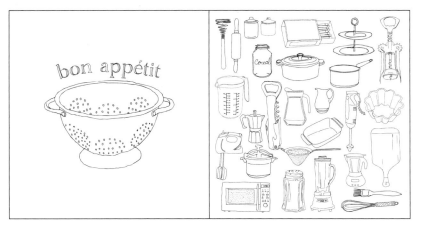

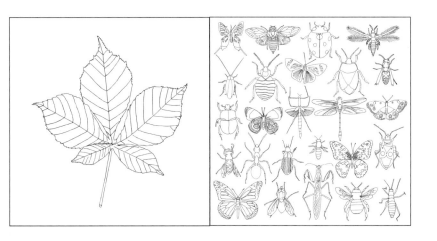

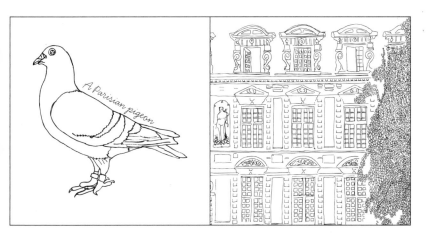

my little haberdashery

BOINH
FRANCE

A small cup of tea?

AU PRINTEMPS

BONJOUR

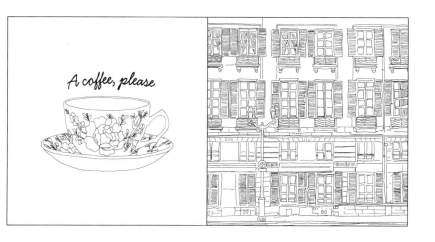

MOULIN ROUGE

La vie en Rose

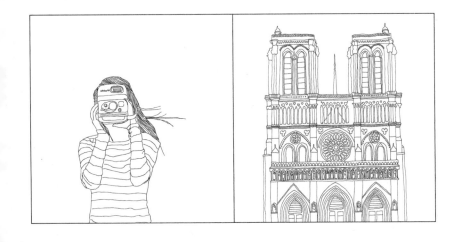